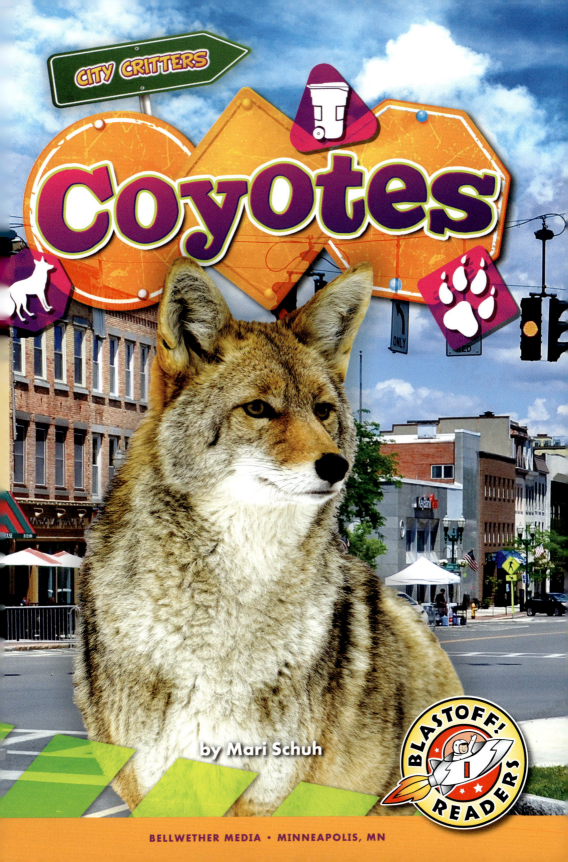

Blastoff! Readers are carefully developed by literacy experts to build reading stamina and move students toward fluency by combining standards-based content with developmentally appropriate text.

Level 1 provides the most support through repetition of high-frequency words, light text, predictable sentence patterns, and strong visual support.

Level 2 offers early readers a bit more challenge through varied sentences, increased text load, and text-supportive special features.

Level 3 advances early-fluent readers toward fluency through increased text load, less reliance on photos, advancing concepts, longer sentences, and more complex special features.

★ Blastoff! Universe

This edition first published in 2026 by Bellwether Media, Inc.

No part of this publication may be reproduced in whole or in part without written permission of the publisher. For information regarding permission, write to Bellwether Media, Inc., Attention: Permissions Department, 3500 American Blvd W, Suite 150, Bloomington, MN 55431.

Library of Congress Cataloging-in-Publication Data

LC record for Coyotes available at: https://lccn.loc.gov/2025012859

Text copyright © 2026 by Bellwether Media, Inc. BLASTOFF! READERS and associated logos are trademarks and/or registered trademarks of Bellwether Media, Inc. Bellwether Media is a division of FlutterBee Education Group.

Editor: Betsy Rathburn   Designer: Gabriel Hilger

Printed in the United States of America, North Mankato, MN.

Table of Contents

What Are Coyotes?	4
Coyotes in the City	10
Coyotes and People	18
Glossary	22
To Learn More	23
Index	24

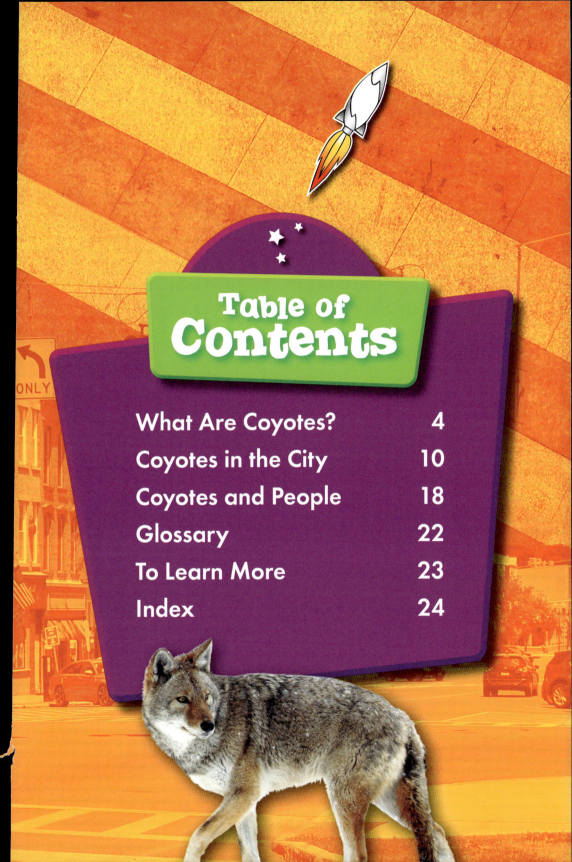

What Are Coyotes?

Coyotes are smart **canines**. They live in many cities.

Coyotes have thick fur. It is tan and gray.

Their fluffy tails point down. Their tails often have a black tip.

Coyotes in the City

Coyotes **adapt** well. They make homes in parks and under decks.

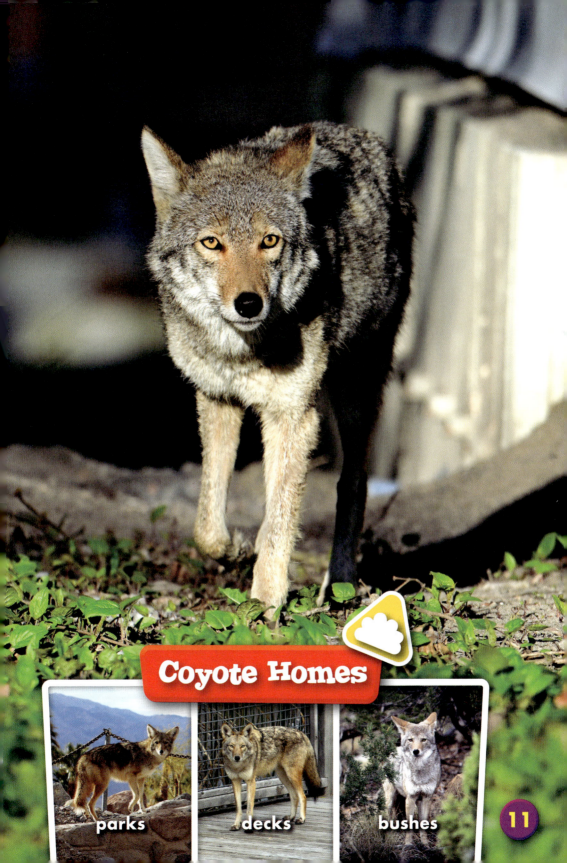

Coyote Homes

parks

decks

bushes

11

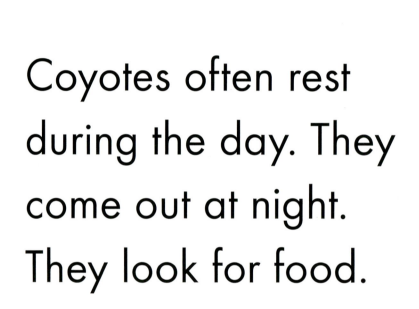

Coyotes often rest during the day. They come out at night. They look for food.

Coyotes hunt in parks. They follow **prey** closely. Then, they **pounce**!

pouncing

prey

Coyotes also find food near roads. They eat rabbits, deer, and fruit.

Coyote Food

rabbits   deer   fruit

Coyotes and People

Coyotes sometimes bother people. They scare pets. They take food from trash bins.

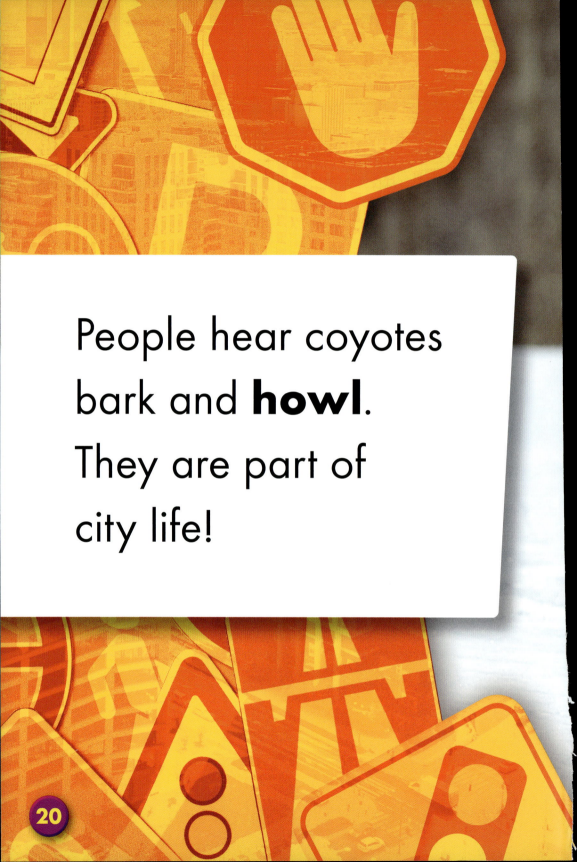

People hear coyotes bark and **howl**. They are part of city life!

Glossary

adapt

to change to fit different conditions

pounce
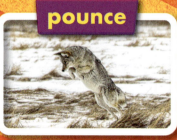
to suddenly jump on something

canines
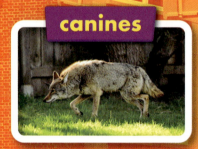
dogs and animals that are related to dogs

prey
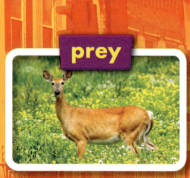
animals that are hunted by other animals for food

howl
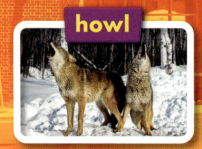
to make a long, loud cry

To Learn More

AT THE LIBRARY

Bolte, Mari. *Coyotes*. Mankato, Minn.: Creative Education and Creative Paperbacks, 2025.

McDonald, Amy. *Coyotes*. Minneapolis, Minn.: Bellwether Media, 2022.

Rains, Dalton. *Coyotes*. Mendota Heights, Minn.: Focus Readers, 2025.

ON THE WEB

FACTSURFER

Factsurfer.com gives you a safe, fun way to find more information.

1. Go to www.factsurfer.com.

2. Enter "coyotes" into the search box and click 🔍.

3. Select your book cover to see a list of related content.

Index

adapt, 10
bark, 20
canines, 4
cities, 4, 20
colors, 6, 8
day, 12
decks, 10
food, 12, 16, 17, 18
fur, 6
homes, 10, 11
howl, 20
hunt, 14
night, 12
parks, 10, 14

people, 18, 20
pets, 18
pounce, 14, 15
prey, 14, 15
rest, 12
roads, 16
tails, 8, 9
trash bins, 18

The images in this book are reproduced through the courtesy of: Jean Landry, front cover (coyote); PQK, front cover (city); Jim Cumming, p. 3; Carol Hamilton, pp. 4-5, 10-11, 22 (canines); annette shaff, pp. 6-7; Jordan Feeg, pp. 8-9; Oblk20, p. 11 (parks); Seyedomid Mostafavi, p. 11 (decks); e, p. 11 (bushes); Peter K. Ziminski, pp. 12-13; Rocky Grimes, pp. 14-15; Kirk Hewlett, p. 15 (prey); kgrif, pp. 16-17; Darren Koobs, p. 17 (rabbits); Terry, p. 17 (deer); Alexandr Blinov, p. 17 (fruit); Matt Knoth, pp. 18-19; outdoorsman, pp. 20-21; Juan Martinez, p. 22 (adapt); Greg Meland, p. 22 (pounce); Jen, p. 22 (prey); hkuchera, p. 22 (howl).